AF454335

WINE

JOHAN MARTIN

WINE
Johan Martin

CARTOONISTS
Bernard Cookson
Břetislav Kovařik
Lubomír Lichý
Jan op de Beeck

HANZESTAD PUBLICATIONS

ISBN
978 907 0506 179

NUR
3447 – 504 – 442 – 370

IMAGES

COCO CHANEL
The Queen of fashion

I drink wine on two occasions:
When I'm in love ...and when I'm not.

Did you know they make anti-wrinkle cream
from grape seeds?

I'm going to hang you, Mireille,
we've already been talking half a bottle.

In 1866, **Pasteur** published *Etudes sur le Vin*, about the diseases of wine. Pasteur demonstrated that yeast was responsible for fermentation to produce alcohol from sugar.
Following his fermentation experiments, Pasteur demonstrated that the skin of grapes was the natural source of yeasts.

LOUIS PASTEUR
French Biologist and Chemist 1822 – 1895

"A bottle of wine contains more Philosophy than all the books in the World."

I've read them all, but it wasn't until I read
this one that I realized: Yes, Henri.....
you're a wine lover.

Cork?

He means a bacterial infection.

Professor **Maynard A. Amerine** 1911 - 1998., University of California, Davis, plant physiology and enology Consultant on many facets of wine, and one of the greatest advocates for California wine. He had a gift for bridging the science and art of winemaking.

MAYNARD A. AMARINE
Wine Science

Drink wine, not labels.

Start pouring idiot!
We don't spend it all evening!

Yes, splendid label.

The winery achieved significant international recognition in 1976, four years after its establishment, at the Judgment of Paris where its 1973 vintage Cabernet Sauvignon won first place among ten top French and California red wines in a blind tasting by leading French wine experts.

Warren Winiarski
FROM PARIS WITH LOVE!
Stag's Leap Wine Cellars

Of course, I can maintain that diet.
No Napa gets trickier.

VINE
EXCLUSIVE

ROBERT PARKER
The Wine Advocate

Thanks for following me.....
and the wine prices!

This is not the year of the wine honey.
It's the price.

WINEBAR 111
21+
90+

Michel Rolland's teacher **Professor Emile Peynod** said: "Only use perfect grapes for a geat wine." Otherwise spoken: It all happens in the vineyard. Emile Peynod introduced Macération à froid in Bordeaux. Cold soaking of the grapes to extract all the skins have to offer: Color, flavors, tannins, and more than a hundred other phenolic materials. Michel Rolland continues a rich tradition. He advises wineries, worldwide.

MICHEL ROLLAND
The flying enologist

"you never, never make good wine
from bad grapes."

According to Professor Peynaud
dentures can be a hindrance to wine tasting.

The difference between these wines?
Eight dollars Signora.

JANCIS ROBINSON
.com

I taste 120 samples a week. I work my ass off, and
he won't even take the empty bottles to the bin.

He's an excellent taster, he can name the year,
the château, and...the new owner.

We also
sell
non-alcoholic
wine.
Why ???

It takes 15 years for a top Bordeaux to develop its nose. Anything you smell before then, well, I'd switch deodorants

Lynch Bages 2018?
I gave him 14 days, not 14 years.

We close in 15 minutes.

Cros Parentoux, a small steep vineyard above grand cru Richebourg, was considered too much work and not worth bothering. The soil is rocky and poor. The climat is rather cold. Henry Jayer who studied enology at the University of Dijon thought otherwise. From 1950 - 2012 he made a top domain of Cros Parentoux.

HENRI JAYER
Roi de Bourgogne 1922 – 2006

I dit it my way.

ALLEN MEADOWS
Burghound

How not to drown
in all those domains in Burgundy?

ROBERT PARKER
The Wine Advocate

ERIC ASIMOV
New York Times

For me Beaujolais Nouveau
is a long, long time ago!

Number 1, was a jolly wine but from
number 7, it became seriously vinous stuff.

83 Points???

Two years ago you also gave it 83 Points.

ALEXANDRE DUMAS
French Author

"Wine – the intellectual part of the meal."

Could you cook tonight Jeff?

MICHEL BETTANE
Classicist and Wine writer Betanne et Desseauve

"Wine is a terrible foe, hard to wrestle with."
Euripides

This is not the right candidate for our Christmas box. May God protect all other boxes as well.

A wine from the year zero.

PARACELSUS
Philip van Hohenheim
Swiss alchemist, physician and astrologer.
1493 – 1541

Whether wine is nourishment,

medicine or poison is a matter of dose.

CELLAR TRACKER
Eric LeVine

That seems like a healthy wine!

He said I did not need antidepressants,
as long as three glasses got me through the day.

OLAVERRI

Wine Merchant and Wine poet
in Pamplona – Spain

Wine is the only Artwork you can drink.

He comes all the way to live
with a glass of good wine.

John Bradley
WINE
IMPORTERS

And this one? Is that also a good wine?

Residents of Vatican City drink 76 bottles of
wine a year. That does not surpise me.

VÁCLAV HAVEL

Czech statesman, author, poet

In politics, it's like wine. Only afterward do you realize wich bottles you have chosen.

JEAN-CLAUDE JUNCKER
President of the European Commission
2014 – 2019

.....and may climate not change the wine.

WAR ON DRUGS

Mind you, he has been trained to detect weed, cork and coke.

"Men are like wine:
some turn to vinegar, but the best
improve with age."

St. EMILION
St. ESTEPHE
St. JULIEN

And now,
can you also make it water again?

JEFF LEVE
The Wine Cellar Insider

Another five Wine Societies to go to.

Galileo Galilei, who lived from 1564 –1642 said:
"Wine is sunlight, held toghether by water."

NUITS
ST. GEORGE

Of course, you may return these,
as long as they're unopened.

BOOKS/EPUBS

At your bookshop

POSTERS

www.etsy.com/shop/JOHANMARTINCARTOONS

MORE CARTOONS

JOHANMARTINCARTOONS.COM